I0461433

The Rescue Story

A Breakthrough With Christ

Patrick James Norman

REDEEMED GRACE PUBLICATIONS

Title: The Rescue Story

Author: Patrick James Norman

First Edition: 2025

Published in: Jemison, Alabama

Scripture References:

THE RESCUE STORY

Cover Design & Interior Layout: Redeemed Grace Publications

ISBN: 979-8-9933916-0-1

CONTENTS

FORWARD

by Phil Perdue

August 2006 – Mission Trip to Ecuador

I n the sweltering summer of 2006, I embarked on a transformative journey—a church mission trip to the heart of Ecuador.

The moment we stepped off the plane, the world felt alive, with sounds foreign yet mesmerizing. Unlike the comforting silence of home, Ecuador's air vibrated with the incessant buzzing of insects, melodious calls of exotic birds, and the ceaseless hum of life pulsating through dense rainforests and sprawling mountains.

We were a team of seven: five determined men from Alabama, a devoted local missionary, an elder Shuar woman with eyes as old as time, and a boy around twelve whose silence spoke volumes. His gaze carried the weight of unspoken stories, deep and haunting, a stark contrast to his youthful face.

Our destination was a secluded Shuar village nestled deep within the formidable Andes. A local villager warned, "The path ahead is treacherous. Walking will take six relentless hours." But our mission fueled us. We climbed into a rickety vehicle, its tires gripping the uneven, narrow roads carving through the towering mountains. Yet, even the vehicle could not conquer the wild entirely. Eventually, we had to continue on foot.

We reached what seemed like a deceptively serene trail—a narrow ledge etched alongside a steep, unforgiving descent. The ground beneath our boots was slick with thick, oozing mud. One misplaced step, one moment of distraction, could mean plummeting into the abyss below. Every breath felt heavier, every heartbeat louder as we trudged forward, acutely aware of the peril lurking with each step.

Then it happened.

I paused, instinctively counting heads. One was missing.

Panic surged instantly. I scanned the slope—and there he was. One of our brothers was trapped, ensnared by the treacherous mud that had swallowed his legs up to the knees. His hiking stick splintered under pressure, and his heavy pack anchored him deeper into the muck. Fear distorted his face. His voice, raw with desperation, echoed through the trees, "Leave me! I'll figure it out! Don't risk it!"

But we couldn't. We wouldn't.

Another brother and I lunged down the slippery slope, adrenaline fueling every frantic movement. Our boots sank with every step, the thick jungle mud trying to claim us as well. I grabbed his pack, pulling with all my might. Our hands clawed at the earth, fingers scraping against roots, rocks, anything to gain leverage. My silent prayers blended with the chaotic symphony of labored breaths and pounding hearts.

Then she appeared.

The elderly Shuar woman, barefoot, her presence both fragile and fierce, descended with grace that defied the treacherous terrain. She said nothing. Her eyes, deep wells of wisdom and calm, met mine. She gestured towards my backpack, lifted it effortlessly despite her frail frame, sprinted up the incline, dropped it, and returned without hesitation.

She knelt beside our trapped brother, her hands gentle, her voice soft yet commanding. Her words, though foreign to our ears, wrapped around him like a balm, calming his frantic cries. Her serenity was a beacon, cutting through the fog of fear that had engulfed us.

With renewed vigor, we dug deeper, our hands blistered and trembling. Finally, with a collective surge, we freed him. He staggered onto solid ground, legs trembling, face pale, eyes glazed with the remnants of terror. But we weren't done.

The ascent back up was brutal. The slope mocked us, steep and slick, daring us to fail. We gripped saplings, our fingers digging into the earth, dragging ourselves upward. She led the way, her movements fluid, her steps deliberate. She turned, her gaze locking onto our exhausted brother. Gesturing from his eyes to her feet, she silently instructed, "Watch me. Follow my steps."

And then it clicked.

Each step she took was a testament to unshaken faith and resilience. Our brother mimicked her movements, stumbling at first, but gradually finding his rhythm. His focus sharpened, his footing steadied. Step by painstaking step, he ascended, until finally, he reached the summit.

We collapsed amidst the towering giants of the rainforest, the ancient trees standing as silent witnesses to our struggle and triumph. The jungle, once deafening with life, now held a sacred stillness. In that profound silence, I felt Him.

Not in a thunderous proclamation or blinding light, but in the quiet presence of a humble Shuar woman.

God spoke—not through words etched in stone or sermons preached from pulpits—but through the tender strength of a stranger's hands, the unwavering calm in her eyes, the silent guidance in her footsteps.

"I am still here," His voice echoed within me. "Not bound by walls or confined to sacred texts. I am here—in the sweat of your brow, the exhaustion in your bones, the desperation in your cries. I am here, in the hands that lift you, the voices that soothe you, the feet that guide you."

Our brother had been trapped—not just in mud, but in life, entangled by the illusion of self-sufficiency, relying on tools that broke under pressure. We tried to save him, bearing his burden, but our strength alone was insufficient. It was when we surrendered, when we cried out, that help arrived—not in the form we expected, but through the one we least anticipated.

That day, eternity unfolded in the middle of an Ecuadorian jungle. The lesson etched into our hearts was simple yet profound:

Jesus is not confined to scriptures or sanctuaries. He breathes in every struggle, every whispered prayer, every act of kindness, no matter how small. He reaches us through the unexpected—a barefoot woman, a gentle word, a steady hand.

True breakthroughs happen when we relinquish our illusions of control, when we look beyond our limited perceptions, and recognize His presence woven into the fabric of our ordinary lives.

God is in the mud, the struggle, the triumph. He is in the people we overlook, the moments we dismiss, the faces of strangers who become saviors.

We reached the mountaintop that day—not just physically, but spiritually.

And even when we stumble, even when we falter, He waits, His hand extended, ready to guide us home.

In a foreign land, beneath an ancient canopy, I saw Jesus—not in visions or dreams, but in the living, breathing spirit of a woman whose name I may never know. Her presence etched an eternal truth into my soul:

God is always present—in every heartbeat, every tear, every act of love. Breakthrough isn't always dramatic; sometimes, it's a quiet nudge, a steady hand, a path illuminated by the simple act of following the footsteps of grace.

In The Rescue Story, you embark on an intimate journey woven with threads of profound joy and deep pain. This book presents more than just a collection of real-life experiences; it testifies to the resilience of the human spirit and the transformative power of faith. Each story highlights the highs and lows that many of us face, drawing you into a tapestry of heartfelt moments that reflect our shared struggles and triumphs. These narratives go beyond tales of hardship or celebration—they mark milestones on the path to discovering something greater than ourselves.

The heart of The Rescue Story invites you to find your breakthrough in Jesus Christ. Whether you stand on the mountaintop of victory or navigate the valleys of despair, this book offers hope and guidance toward your breakthrough. It speaks directly to your soul's deepest longing for connection, healing, and purpose. As you turn each page, may you find inspiration, comfort, and the unshakable truth that in both your brightest joys and darkest pains, Jesus remains present, ready to rescue, restore, and renew.

INTRODUCTION

Where do you find hope when life feels overwhelming? Where do you find peace when everything seems to be falling apart? Who do you turn to when you're in desperate need of comfort and direction? I've wrestled with these questions myself, and while I didn't always know the answers,

I've found clarity over time. Now, I want to help you find that same clarity for yourself.

Life is a journey, isn't it? It's filled with soaring highs and crushing lows—moments when everything feels crystal clear and seasons when confusion clouds our hearts. Each of us carries a story: some chapters filled with beauty, others marked by brokenness. But here's the thing—no story is beyond redemption. That's what The Rescue Story is all about. It's an invitation to discover the overwhelming and never-ending love of Jesus Christ. This isn't about what we've accomplished, who we know, or even how "good" we've been. It's about understanding that Christ's grace is what truly rescues us. Not our achievements, not our relationships, not even our own efforts—just His grace.

As you flip through these pages, you'll come face-to-face with a message that can transform your life: Jesus alone is the way to heaven. His life, His death, and His resurrection aren't just distant historical facts—they're divine acts of love, personally meant for you. Wherever life finds you today—whether you're celebrating a victory or nursing a heartbreak—Jesus is right there, arms wide open, offering you the gift of salvation. This isn't about religious rituals or checking spiritual boxes; it's about a real, authentic relationship with the One who gave everything to rescue you.

I know how easy it is to let the pain and hardships we've faced define us. But here's the truth: our experiences, both joyful and painful, are tools that can draw us closer to God. They shape who we are, refine our hearts, and plant seeds of faith not just in us, but in the people around us. In this book, you'll read stories of people who found God's light shining the brightest in their darkest moments. You'll see how even the most broken parts of our lives can reflect His grace.

And if you're feeling lost, burdened, or like you're on the brink of a breakdown as you read this, please hear me—sometimes, a breakdown is exactly what leads to a breakthrough with Christ. It's in those raw, vulnerable spaces where we often hear His voice the clearest. When we finally come to the end of ourselves, that's when we truly discover the beginning of His grace. No pit is too deep, no heart too shattered for Jesus to reach in and rescue.

Throughout these chapters, you'll see that faith—not perfection—is what brings salvation. Jesus didn't die on the cross because we earned it. He did it to offer us a gift we could never deserve, one we can only receive through His grace. Accepting this gift doesn't mean life will be free of struggles, but it does mean you'll never have to face those struggles alone. God will use your past, your pain, and even your passions to draw your heart—and the hearts of others—closer to Him.

I want to be honest with you: I'm not a Bible scholar. I don't have all the answers. But I do know who created me, and I know who I belong to. That truth is rock-solid in my heart, and it's what drives me to share the good news of Jesus Christ. This isn't about theology or complex doctrines; it's about the undeniable presence of a Savior who changed my life—and can change yours too.

At the core of it all, my hope is simple. I want to reach into the places where hope feels absent and remind you that you are not alone in this world. Because Christ overcame death, you can overcome the trials, fears, and burdens that weigh you down. The Rescue Story isn't just words on a page; it's a message that echoes into eternity, calling your name. Welcome to this journey of hope, healing, and the greatest rescue story ever told.

CHAPTER 1

THE RESCUE

"For the Son of Man came to seek and to save the lost." — Luke 19:10

When you really think about it, those words carry a powerful echo, resonating through every moment in history and piercing the darkness with an unyielding light. Picture the weight of humanity's despair—crushing, suffocating—bound by chains of sin, drowning in hopelessness. Imagine the silent cries of countless hearts aching for redemption, drifting upward like smoke. But here's the thing: heaven doesn't stay silent. The King of Glory rises with a mission etched into eternity—a divine rescue unlike anything the world has ever seen.

This story isn't a quiet whisper; it roars to life like a lion. Jesus, the Son of God, steps into the mess of human history. He doesn't come with legions of angels or the pomp of royal decrees. Instead, He's wrapped in fragile flesh, born in the obscurity of a manger. Every heartbeat of His life echoes the rhythm of rescue—through miracles, words of truth, and every drop of blood spilled on the dusty roads of Judea. This isn't passive love; it's relentless pursuit. It's light clashing with darkness, reaching its peak as the Savior walks, undeterred, toward the ultimate battleground: the cross.

Can you feel that weight? The tension rising as the enemy recoils. Demons tremble at His name; storms quiet at His command. The weight of the world's sin presses down on His shoulders, yet His gaze never wavers. No hesitation. No retreat. The Lamb of God willingly embraces the agony of crucifixion because this rescue—it's personal. It's for you. It's for me. When He cries out, "It is finished," it's not the faint whisper of defeat but a triumphant roar that shatters the chains of death and hell.

But this isn't just an ancient tale confined to dusty pages. It's a living, breathing testament of divine love and power. As you read this, prepare your heart. You're about to encounter the fierce, unstoppable force of a Savior who didn't just come to offer hope—He came to guarantee it. Are you ready to be changed?

Now, picture a man standing at a cross-roads, much like the rich young ruler who once approached Jesus. This man has every-thing—status, possessions, influence—but his heart is restless. He's searching, craving an eternal security that money can't buy. Jesus tells him to let go of his treasures and fol-low Him, but the man walks away, sad. Not because he's poor, but because he's weighed down by his own heart. And isn't that us sometimes? Clutching tightly to our own ver-sions of security, blind to the rescue Jesus of-fers.

Even Jesus' closest friends struggled to understand His mission. In Matthew 20, Jesus tells His disciples—again—what's coming: betrayal, condemnation, mockery, scourging, crucifixion, and resurrection. But they just don't get it. They're picturing thrones and crowns, not salvation through a cross. Their misunderstanding isn't so different from ours. We expect rescue to look victorious, not sacrificial.

But here's the thing: the crucifixion isn't a tragic end. It's the heart of the rescue plan. On that cross, Jesus carries all of humanity's brokenness—not just our sins, but the deep fractures in our souls. His death tears down the barriers between us and God—barriers we built with pride, fear, and self-reliance. And without the resurrection, His death would be just another sad story. But the empty tomb? It's proof that death doesn't get the final word.

Think about this: without light, darkness has no definition. Without good, evil lacks contrast. Jesus is that light and goodness. He doesn't come to tweak behaviors or polish appearances; He comes to transform us from the inside out. This isn't self-improvement.

It's rescue—from sin, from death, and from ourselves.

Remember the criminal hanging beside Jesus on the cross? In unimaginable agony, this man acknowledges his guilt and turns to Jesus in faith. He admits his wrongs, defends Jesus' innocence, and simply asks to be remembered. And Jesus, with boundless grace, says, "Truly I tell you, today you will be with me in paradise." That moment shouts the truth: salvation isn't earned through deeds. It's a gift of grace, received through faith.

The rescue story of Jesus Christ is the centerpiece of our faith. It's God's relentless pursuit of humanity. Galatians 4:4-5 says, "But when the fullness of time had come, God sent forth his Son... to redeem those who were under the law, so that we might receive adoption as sons." This was the plan all along—a divine rescue mission, meticulously crafted, fueled by God's unwavering love.

Jesus' life on Earth? It was filled with powerful teachings, miracles, and compassion. He preached the coming of God's Kingdom, calling people to repentance and faith. Luke 19:10 sums it up: "For the Son of Man came to seek and to save the lost." His actions reflected the heart of God, reaching out to the broken, offering hope.

The climax? The Passion of Christ. Betrayed, arrested, falsely accused, beaten—Jesus faced it all without flinching. Isaiah 53:5 says, "He was pierced for our transgressions... and with His wounds we are healed." His suffering wasn't pointless. It was the very means of our salvation.

On the cross, Jesus bore our sins. When He declared, "It is finished," it wasn't defeat. It was victory. The debt was paid in full. His death satisfied divine justice, making reconciliation with God possible.

But the story doesn't end there. Three days later, Jesus rose from the grave, defeating sin and death. 1 Corinthians 15:20-22 proclaims, "Christ has been raised from the dead... as in Adam all die, so also in Christ shall all be made alive." The resurrection isn't just a footnote; it's the cornerstone of our faith.

And the rescue mission isn't over. Jesus commissions us to spread the good news. Matthew 28:19-20 says, "Go therefore and make disciples of all nations... teaching them to observe all that I have commanded you." Empowered by the Holy Spirit, we're called to be His ambassadors, sharing the invitation of salvation with the world.

This story isn't just history. It's a living reality, transforming lives every day. It's the ultimate expression of God's love and power, calling each of us to respond with faith and gratitude.

Jesus said, "I am the way, the truth, and the life." That's not just a metaphor. He's the map, the compass, and the destination. His way leads us home, His truth sets us free, and His life breathes eternity into our hearts. This is the Gospel—a love so relentless, it defeats death to rescue us all.

Jesus is "The Rescue Story" because His life, death, and resurrection embody the ultimate act of divine intervention and love. He stepped into the mess of our brokenness, not as a distant observer but as an active Savior, carrying the weight of our sins and offering a path to redemption. His sacrifice on the cross wasn't just an event in history—it was the turning point for humanity, where grace triumphed over judgment and life conquered death.

Through His resurrection, He shattered the chains of sin and opened the door to eternal life. This isn't just a story we read; it's the living, breathing truth that transforms hearts and restores souls. Jesus doesn't merely offer rescue; He is the Rescue—our hope, our salvation, and the anchor for every soul seeking light in the darkness.

Chapter 2

Identity In Christ

Discovering who you truly are doesn't come from what the world says about you. It emerges from the unchanging truth found in Christ. As 2 Corinthians 5:17 says, "Therefore, if anyone is in Christ, he is a new creation; the old has passed away, behold, the new has come." This isn't a passive shift—it's a powerful, divine transformation that rewrites your very core. You're not defined by fleeting affirmations from society. Instead, your life flourishes in the victory Christ secured for you. Every breath you take carries purpose, crafted by the One who knew you before time began.

In a world filled with loud, competing voices trying to mold you, it's crucial to anchor yourself in a deeper truth. While society pushes you to fit into temporary ideals, there's a gentle, persistent voice calling you by name. Isaiah 43:1 reminds us, "I have called you by name; you are Mine." This is more than comforting words—it's an eternal truth sealed by Christ's love and sacrifice. When doubts creep in, threatening your sense of self, Christ's declaration remains unshaken. Your identity isn't fragile; it's a stronghold built upon an unmovable foundation.

Think about the Apostle Paul. He once found his worth in his status and achievements. But everything changed when he encountered Christ. He declared, "I have been crucified with Christ; it is no longer I who live, but Christ lives in me" (Galatians 2:20). Those worldly accomplishments faded in the light of his new identity in Christ. For Paul, identity wasn't an add-on; it became the source of his life. His past mistakes and fears were left at the cross, and what emerged was a life transformed, rooted deeply in God.

This journey of discovering identity isn't without challenges. The enemy constantly tries to confuse and distract us, whispering lies that we're defined by our failures or fears. But Scripture cuts through those lies. 1 Peter 2:9 boldly states, "You are a chosen race, a royal priesthood, a holy nation, a people for His own possession." This isn't just uplifting—it's the truth. When you truly embrace who you are in Christ, Scripture doesn't just inform you—it ignites you. You're not who the world says you are. You're who Christ says you are: redeemed, restored, and deeply loved.

Identity isn't just about where you're born or the titles you hold. It's shaped by experiences, relationships, and the environments you're part of. And while these things influence you, they don't define you. Your true essence comes from Christ.

I've thought a lot about this in my own life. I married my best friend seven years ago, and together we're raising three wonderful kids.

Even in the joy of these roles, I've found myself asking, "Who am I beyond my achievements and responsibilities?" This question has been a turning point, especially in my roles as a husband and father. It's in the quiet, reflective moments that I've faced truths I often avoid. There's nothing more humbling than confronting realities you'd rather ignore.

Interestingly, I didn't face this question because of a crisis. I simply realized it was time to stop living outwardly and start looking inward. I needed to stop defining my worth by what I do and start understanding who I am in Christ.

Growing up, I was deeply involved in church—Sunday services, midweek gatherings, camps, choir practices—you name it. It felt like home. I knew Bible stories, sang the songs, and recited prayers. But being in church didn't automatically mean I understood my identity in Christ. I had knowledge about Jesus, but that's different from knowing who I am because of Him. My faith was present, but it lacked depth. Without genuine connection, words lose their meaning.

For a long time, I approached faith out of obligation, as if God had assigned me tasks to complete. But through learning and reflection, I've come to see that faith isn't about chores; it's about the heart behind every word and action. It's about a relationship with God. I realized I'd been trying to earn what God freely gave. Now, I live in that gift, sharing the truth I've discovered: Jesus is the answer, the one who rescues us all.

In my daily life, I juggle many roles—husband, dad, leader. I manage teams, solve problems, and carry responsibilities seriously, striving to be dependable and hardworking. But none of these roles define me. They're parts of my life, but not my core identity. At my core is something quieter, eternal, and unchanging. It's the unshakeable truth that I belong to God.

Basing our identity on roles can be risky because when those roles change, we might feel lost. But when rooted in Christ, our sense of self remains anchored, even in life's storms.

I've experienced spiritual drifting—going through the motions, praying without heart, reading Scripture mechanically. Drifting happens subtly, masked by routine. It's even possible to seem faithful outwardly while feeling disconnected inside.

I realized I was drifting during a simple car ride. I turned off the radio, and a question surfaced: "Am I truly living for Jesus, and do my actions reflect that?" It wasn't self-pity; it was honest reflection. My family depends on me, and I wondered if I was leading them well. The truth was hard to face—I had drifted from Jesus. That realization became a turning point.

Around that time, I began writing. Talking about the Gospel was challenging, but writing helped me express what was in my heart.

This practice deepened my faith and led me to become a Christian author.

One of the hardest lessons was letting go of the idea that I needed to earn Jesus' love. I thought more prayers and better behavior would make me worthy. But our connection with Christ isn't earned; it's already established. We simply need to embrace it. It's not about performing; it's about resting in who He is.

When Scripture shifts from being a task to a living, breathing guide, faith comes alive. It stops feeling like an obligation and starts feeling like a privilege. Immersing ourselves in God's Word opens our hearts, cultivating wisdom, compassion, and courage to share our faith authentically.

Reflecting on my journey allows me to share lessons learned, understanding that even my struggles can be meaningful to others. We all walk different paths, but God's purpose for each of us holds significance. Recognizing this freed me from the trap of comparison. It's not about having all the answers; it's about pointing back to Christ's grace through our experiences.

Knowing who you are in Christ frees you from the chase for approval and the fear of failure. Your identity isn't tied to your past or performance but anchored in an unchanging God.

I've been blessed by others' faith too. Years ago, I met a Jiu-Jitsu instructor whose quiet, steady faith in Christ inspired me. I didn't earn a black belt, but I gained confidence and learned the importance of encouragement and perseverance. His genuine faith showed me that failure isn't something to fear—it's part of growth.

I see my life like a Jiu-Jitsu Gi, stitched together with moments, memories, mistakes, and miracles. Joy and pain woven together, creating a story that matters. Christ holds it all, making even the broken parts beautiful.

Relationships shape our identity. When we live from our identity in Christ, we inspire others to do the same. That's what I aim to do through writing—not because I'm an expert, but because I've experienced God's grace firsthand.

This isn't about religion; it's about a relationship with God. It's about coming home to who I truly am—a believer, a son, a vessel of grace. I used to think I had to build my identity, but now I know it's a gift I receive. Jesus' sacrifice secured that for all of us. Identity isn't something we achieve; it's a promise we embrace. And that truth applies to you, too.

Take a moment to reflect: What is your true identity? Are you shaping your life around the temporary values of the world, chasing after fleeting approval, status, and accomplishments? Or are you living for Jesus, anchoring your heart in His eternal truth and grace? It's easy to get caught up in the noise of expectations, but deep inside, there's a question waiting to be answered—Who am I beyond what I do, beyond what others say? Are your choices, priorities, and passions rooted in the unchanging love of Christ, or are they driven by the world's shifting standards? Pause and consider—where does your identity truly lie?

CHAPTER 3

MY BEGINNING

In the beginning, a voice thundered through the void, shaking the silence into existence. The earth was formless, and darkness veiled the deep. Yet amid the vast emptiness, the Spirit of God hovered over the waters, poised with purpose. Then God spoke,

'Let there be light,' and light pierced the darkness, igniting the first spark of revelation. This was the genesis of all things—the foundation where faith took root.

Faith began not as a whisper but as a declaration, bold and commanding. It surged forth from the very words of God, breathing life into lifelessness, order into chaos. In the brilliance of that first light, humanity's journey toward understanding the unseen commenced. Each heartbeat, each breath, echoes the rhythm of that divine command. Here lies the beginning of faith: not in the quiet corners of doubt, but in the resounding certainty of God's voice breaking into the void.

My faith took root in my Grandmother's living room, not a church pew. She lived her unwavering love for Jesus through her daily life—folding laundry, praying quietly, and carrying peace into every room. She didn't preach; she demonstrated faith right beside me, and that was enough.

Grandmother's faith was gentle. She read the Bible to me before bed, and we'd play games selecting random Bible passages. Her faith never shouted, but it echoed through her actions and approach to everything.

My mom embodied a different kind of faith—bold, passionate, and deeply committed. She didn't just believe in Jesus; she wrestled with Him. Her faith wasn't calm, especially when her health declined. She questioned, expressed frustration, and experienced tension, but she never let go. She clung to Jesus with everything she had, even when it hurt.

I witnessed her struggle—physically and spiritually. Her prayers resembled heartfelt arguments, and her passion often spilled into pain. But that was her way: authentic, raw, and real. She never faked it; she brought her whole self to God. That vulnerability strengthened her faith, teaching me that faith isn't always neat; it can be loud, messy, and emotional. Yet, it remains faithful. Her love for Jesus wasn't about comfort; it was about honesty, even in chaos. That kind of faith shaped my walk with God more profoundly than any sermon ever could.

When my mother passed unexpectedly, I sat with Dad in the living room. Shaken, not just fearful but profoundly broken, he looked lost. I had performed CPR, but she was gone. After her journey ended, I saw Dad collapse emotionally and spiritually—the steady, strong man suddenly quiet and withdrawn. For the first time, he had no direction or answers.

Living with him mattered more than I realized. I didn't have words to fix anything, but I remained present. Sometimes, presence anchors someone who's drifting. My presence reminded him life wasn't over. Looking back, I know he needed hope.

Soon after, I met my wife, who changed both our lives. She brought light, warmth, and renewal to our family. Watching Dad smile, hope, and believe again felt like spring after a long winter. I genuinely believe God used that season to restore something in him—hope and purpose.

Sometimes, God answers prayers through people. He answered my Dad's when he met my step-mom on the Mississippi coast. Her presence calmed him and brought out his best. She rekindled hope he'd lost. Her gentle love was undeniable. Over time, he transformed—standing taller, feeling softer, shining brighter. Grief gave way to grace. I believe God sent her to heal him, and she needed him too.

Growing up, I attended church weekly with my Grandparents. We sat in the back, near the top—"back row Baptists." My wise and loving Aunt and Uncle joined us, and after church, we'd share lunch, often soup. My grandfather wasn't a fan, but he ate it for us. On Wednesdays, we met after school, ate dinner at church, and attended youth worship. As much as my parents believed in God, my grandparents' influence kept us connected to church.

Understanding my identity in Christ shapes my parenting. I don't just want obedient kids; I want them to believe in Jesus. I want them to feel loved before chasing achievements, to know they're chosen for who they are, and to feel seen even when they feel invisible. This foundation builds character and confidence.

I can't pass on what I haven't embraced. So, I speak identity into my kids—not just rules, but truth. I remind them they're valuable for who they are, not what they do. I assure them they belong, even when they mess up. I model personal faith, not just functional faith.

It's challenging. Even when I feel like I'm winging it, I remember that living from my identity in Christ gives my kids a solid foundation—presence, not control. They'll remember who their parents are, who they are, and what God can do.

Identity provides direction, like a compass pointing home. It guides us, but following it remains the challenge.

This clarity transforms my reading, writing, and decision-making. I ask, "What aligns with who I am in Christ?" not "What looks good?" This shift saves me from burnout, comparison, and chasing meaningless things. It helps me say no to distractions and yes to purpose.

Purpose is powerful. It's about doing what's right, not just what's important.

Life shakes, circumstances change, people disappoint, and plans fall apart. But when your identity is in Christ, storms can't shake your foundation. Jesus has already told us how the story ends.

It's easy to build life on titles, achievements, and relationships, but those shift and fade. Identity in Christ remains eternal and unshakable. Building on that creates something lasting.

Peace comes when you stop trying to earn your place and start living from it. It's steady and effective. Life won't necessarily get easier; your soul will grow quieter. You'll stop striving and start abiding.

Peace transforms how you show up in the world. It frees you from needing to prove yourself or fearing failure. It fosters quiet confidence that doesn't seek applause. Absolute freedom begins here. Peace is calm and stable, not surrender. It shapes your identity.

Understanding your identity in Christ helps you share it with others. People need answers. This understanding allows us to share the truth confidently. It doesn't make us perfect; it makes us real. Perfection feels insincere. People seek something relatable. God's word grounds this identity. We must use our sword.

People are drawn to stability, authenticity, and peace. Our job is to demonstrate Christ's followership. Words without action damage the message and undermine the goal: bringing people to Jesus Christ.

Influence comes from being genuine and intentional. Show up, love well, and stay grounded. Stop trying to change people; invite them to see what's possible. Change is tough—have you tried changing yourself? Faith alone isn't enough; action matters.

Understanding your identity in Christ isn't the end; it's the beginning. It's the starting line of a life lived in truth, power, and peace. It moves you past questioning your identity to living with a clear purpose.

This journey isn't about reaching a destination. It's about waking up and remembering what's already true. That choice changes everything. It's about being truly changed by the Holy Spirit.

Now, ask yourself: Do you know your identity?

CHAPTER 4

My New Calling

Wen Christ calls you, it's not just a gentle tap on the shoulder; it's a life-altering awakening that shakes the very foundation of your existence. It's not simply an invitation—it's a powerful summons that pierces through your soul and ignites an unquenchable fire within. Paul's words in Romans 8:30 capture this beautifully: "And those whom he predestined he also called, and those whom he called he also justified, and those whom he justified he also glorified." This isn't a call you can ignore. It breaks through every barrier—be it sin, fear, or self-doubt—and demands a heartfelt response.

When Christ calls, He asks for your whole heart. It's not a casual, "Hey, if you're free, come follow me." No, it's the same powerful voice that spoke the world into existence, now speaking directly to you: "Follow me"

(Matthew 4:19). This call doesn't just shuffle your daily routine; it transforms your very identity. Think about the fishermen who left their nets, the tax collectors who abandoned their booths, and the sinners who stepped into the light—all because they heard and responded. They weren't defined by their past mistakes or personal goals anymore. They were marked by the purpose Christ had for them.

Answering Christ's call isn't a one-time event; it's a lifelong journey. It's hearing His voice—the Shepherd's voice—amid all the noise and distractions of the world. Jesus said in John 10:27, "My sheep hear my voice, and I know them, and they follow me." This call isn't confined to just a single moment in time. It echoes throughout your life, pulling you into deeper faith, stronger obedience, and a closer relationship with Him. It becomes the heartbeat of your soul, shaping your destiny and anchoring your eternity.

I vividly remember the moment my life changed. I was on a work trip to Houston, Texas—a city I'd never visited before—attending a safety conference. I thought it would be just another professional event, but God had other plans. Amid the hustle and noise of the conference, surrounded by industry professionals, I had an unexpected encounter that would redefine my purpose.

I met this man during a break, and we struck up a conversation. At first, it was light and casual—we talked about diet plans, staying healthy as we got older, and the challenges of maintaining fitness. He shared his struggles with staying active despite his best efforts, and I related by talking about my own journey, mentioning my eight years of on-and-off Jiu-jitsu training. I also shared how a low-carb diet worked best for me, especially since my family has a history of diabetes. We bonded over our personal health experiences without even realizing how much deeper the conversation was about to go.

As we chatted, the topic shifted from health to something far more profound—faith. He opened up about his family's deep involvement in sharing God's love, even mentioning they had a TV show centered around their faith. To my surprise, they'd also appeared in the movie "God's Not Dead." This revelation added a whole new layer to our exchange, weaving spiritual connections into what had started as a simple conversation about fitness.

Feeling inspired, I shared something I'd kept hidden for years—a dream of writing books, especially children's books. I even had an idea for a Christmas story tucked away, gathering dust because I was too afraid to pursue it. I lacked the confidence and know-how to bring it to life. But something about our conversation encouraged me to open up, and his genuine enthusiasm sparked a sense of courage I hadn't felt in a long time.

His words were more than just encouragement; they were a divine nudge. He urged me to take that leap of faith, to stop overthinking and just go for it. His belief in me planted a seed of determination that shifted my entire mindset. Looking back, I know that God orchestrated that meeting as part of His perfect plan.

Fast forward to today, and I'm living that calling. My writing has reached hearts and touched lives in ways I never dreamed possible. People have shared testimonies with me—stories of how my words have inspired them, deepened their faith, and even rekindled their relationship with God. It's humbling, surreal, and profoundly fulfilling.

Churches have even adapted my stories into children's plays, bringing the messages to life in vibrant, heartfelt performances. Watching kids learn about Christ through my work has been an overwhelming blessing. It's a constant reminder that I'm walking the path God designed for me.

But amidst the joy and fulfillment, I'm always careful to guard my heart against pride. The recognition and accolades are fleeting—they aren't the true measure of success. My focus remains on glorifying God, not myself. Every word I write, every story I craft, is a testament to His grace. He's the source of my inspiration, the giver of my talents, and the purpose behind my passion.

Reflecting on that seemingly ordinary work trip to Houston, I see now how God works in the most unexpected ways. A simple conversation about diet and fitness turned into a divine encounter that changed the course of my life. In the midst of the ordinary, I found the extraordinary.

In the end, my journey is a testament to the power of obedience and the beauty of God's perfect timing. Writing and sharing Christ's message isn't just a calling—it's a privilege. And with every word I write, I carry a heart full of gratitude, always remembering that all the glory belongs to Him.

CHAPTER 5

THE ARMOR OF GOD

"**P**ut on the whole armor of God, that you may be able to stand against the schemes of the devil." — Ephesians 6:11 (ESV)

You know, life feels like a battle sometimes—actually, it is a battle. Not the kind you see in movies with swords clashing and armies charging, but a spiritual one that's constantly happening around us, even if we don't always notice. The Apostle Paul wasn't being dramatic when he wrote about this in Ephesians 6:11. He was giving us a wake-up call—a real, urgent plea to suit up with God's armor because whether we like it or not, the enemy is out there, scheming, lurking, waiting for a weak spot.

Imagine this: a soldier steps into a war zone without any armor, no helmet, no shield, nothing. What do you think happens? The enemy doesn't wait around politely—they attack. The same goes for us. If we go through life without God's protection, we're wide open to the enemy's attacks—doubt sneaks in, fear takes root, temptation whispers, and deception clouds our judgment. But when we're wearing God's armor—the belt of truth, the breastplate of righteousness, the shield of faith—those attacks don't stand a chance. Each lie gets crushed by God's truth, each dart of fear is blocked by unwavering faith.

Now, don't think of this armor as just a metaphorical outfit we put on during Sunday service. This isn't decorative; it's battle gear, meant for real-life action. Walking in God's armor isn't about being religious at specific times; it's about being ready in every moment—whether you're at work, dealing with family chaos, or facing personal struggles. The helmet of salvation keeps your mind focused when life gets noisy, and the sword of the Spirit—God's Word—is your offensive weapon, cutting through lies with the sharp edge of truth. We're not relying on our strength here; we're leaning on God's power, fully armed to face whatever comes our way.

Take mornings in my house, for example. They're anything but peaceful—kids scrambling for school, my wife rushing around, tension thick in the air. It's not that we're angry; we're overwhelmed. In those moments, I have to consciously fight for patience. I lean into God's armor, not as some abstract idea but as a real source of strength. I first heard about it at a youth retreat, and it's stuck with me ever since.

Even when I pray, plan, and try my best, I still find myself feeling lost. That's when I realize—strength isn't about having everything under control. It's about showing up, being honest about where I am, embracing peace, and trusting that God's given me exactly what I need to get through. The armor isn't about surviving; it's about thriving, about facing each day with resilience rooted in faith. I want my wife and kids to see that in me—not a perfect man, but a man who stays standing even when life gets tough.

I used to think, "My kid will never act like that." Then my firstborn turned two, and reality hit hard. Suddenly, I was in daily battles over things like "Don't put that in your mouth" or "Where are your shoes?" I'd pray for patience, peace, and love, but some days they felt miles out of reach. I'd wonder, "Why is this so hard? Why can't I handle this better?" Maybe because God doesn't just hand us patience—He gives us opportunities to practice it.

There are days I feel completely unprepared. I fall back into old habits, ignore what I know God's trying to teach me, and then frustration kicks in—not just with the circumstances but with myself. But when I reflect on Paul's letters, written from prison, filled with wisdom born from hardship, or Peter's struggles walking through literal storms, I find courage. They didn't have it all together, and yet their faith carried them. If they needed help, so do I.

I've realized that just enduring isn't enough. I need to actively trust God. Some days, simply saying, "God, I trust you," feels like a victory. When I feel inadequate, I open my Bible—not to check off a box, but to find hope. I'm never meant to face these battles alone. Jesus is my strength.

For years, I thought being strong meant being in control. But after nearly fifteen years working in logistics and management, I've learned that control is an illusion. Life doesn't follow scripts. Adaptability is key. And faith? It's not about controlling outcomes; it's about surrendering control. A mission trip taught me this lesson. I saw how, like water in a creek, God's grace flows through us, shaping us, helping us influence others while simultaneously molding us.

When doubts creep in—doubts about my worth, my ability, God's presence—I find grounding in honesty. Being real with myself and with God keeps me steady. Mornings are when this hits hardest—maybe it's the fatigue or the overwhelming sense of responsibility. But that's when God speaks the clearest, reminding me that I'm not carrying this weight alone.

I remember the day my son came home upset because of a mean kid at school. As a dad, it broke my heart. I wanted to shield him from that pain, but I knew I couldn't. What I could do was prepare him. I thought about Peter—how he faltered yet kept his focus on Jesus. That's how I want to guide my kids: teaching them resilience, not by keeping them from struggles but by walking with them through it.

Every day brings new challenges. Teaching my kids who they are, grounded in faith, means helping them tune out the world's noise. It's not about having all the answers but creating a home where faith feels real, where it's okay to ask hard questions, where we face doubts together.

Regret can be like quicksand, pulling us away from truth. I've been there. But Paul's life shows that even with a past full of mistakes, grace prevails. I find that same grace in small daily choices—choosing prayer over worry, owning up to my mistakes, reaching out when I've hurt someone. This is how resilience grows.

Peace isn't about a conflict-free life. It's about finding calm in the middle of chaos—like holding onto the wheel during a storm. My anxious, sensitive son doesn't need me to have all the answers; he needs my presence, my patience, my listening ear. That's what God gives us, too—His steady presence amid our mess.

Faith isn't a shield that makes problems disappear. It's what helps us face them head-on. Mental battles are the hardest, especially as a parent. I second-guess my decisions, wonder if I'm doing more harm than good. But Scripture reminds me that I'm not defined by my failures. I can learn, grow, and try again.

I need God's Word daily—not just when life gets hard. It's easy to talk about faith when things are smooth, but real faith shows up when life doesn't make sense. Paul called God's Word a weapon, and I believe it. It cuts through the lies we tell ourselves, the doubts that creep in.

I love Peter's story. When he started to sink, Jesus didn't scold him; He reached out His hand. The question is, do we grab it? I've ignored it before, thinking I could handle things on my own. But every time, I've found myself sinking. I've learned that resilience comes from reaching out, every single time.

Prayer stabilizes me. Not fancy prayers—just honest ones. Telling God exactly how I feel makes all the difference. Resilience isn't about getting it right all the time. It's about showing up, speaking truth even when I'm scared, trusting God even when I don't feel strong.

I strive to be honest, even when it's uncomfortable. Temptation doesn't always come in obvious forms. Sometimes it's in the little things—self-pity, pride, the urge to sugarcoat the truth. I've messed up, said things I regret, bent the truth to avoid conflict. But confession keeps me grounded, creates space for grace. My kids don't need a perfect dad—they need one who's real, who admits mistakes, who shows them what humility and growth look like.

Living equipped means staying engaged, asking for help, resisting the urge to grow bitter when life gets tough. I want my kids to see that it's okay to fall, as long as you get back up. That's where resilience is built.

Daily choices matter. Choosing prayer instead of panic, truth instead of lies, peace instead of conflict—these small decisions shape us. They build a strength that lasts, helping us move from just surviving to truly standing firm. Being real about my struggles doesn't make me weak; it shows the courage growing inside me. And if I can find that courage, so can you.

God's support doesn't waver. Through honesty, calmness, trust, and purposeful words, I find my footing. As a father, a mentor, and a believer, I choose courage over fear. I speak life into my home. I grow a faith that's real and enduring. I won't be perfect—and that's okay. My kids don't need perfection; they need to see someone trying, someone leaning on God's armor, not to appear strong, but to truly live strong.

The Armor of God isn't just a concept; it's my spiritual defense:

The Belt of Truth keeps me grounded when lies press in.

The Breastplate of Righteousness guards my heart, reminding me that what I do matters.

The Shoes of Peace help me stand firm and spread hope wherever I go.

The Shield of Faith blocks the arrows of doubt, fear, and frustration.

The Helmet of Salvation protects my mind, helping me stay clear-headed when life feels overwhelming.

The Sword of the Spirit—God's Word—is my weapon, cutting through darkness with truth.

And every day, I choose to put it on. Not because I'm strong, but because I know where my strength comes from.

CHAPTER 6

OUR ENEMY'S TACTICS

I magine life as a battlefield—not one filled with swords and shields, but with invisible forces fighting for our hearts and minds. The Apostle Paul puts it clearly in Ephesians 6:12: "For we do not wrestle against flesh and blood, but against the rulers, against the authorities, against the cosmic powers over this present darkness, against the spiritual forces of evil in the heavenly places." This battle isn't physical; the enemy uses tactics that are cunning and relentless, hiding in the shadows and feeding off our ignorance and complacency.

One of the enemy's most powerful weapons is fear. It's not just an emotion but a tool used to paralyze our faith. Peter warned us in 1 Peter 5:8, "Be sober-minded; be watchful. Your adversary the devil prowls around like a roaring lion, seeking someone to devour." Fear makes our problems look bigger than they really are, convincing us that we're alone in our struggles. It isolates us, cutting off the support we'd get from our communities, leaving us feeling helpless.

Temptation is another strategy in the enemy's playbook. James 1:14-15 explains how it works: "But each person is tempted when he is lured and enticed by his own desire. Then desire when it has conceived gives birth to sin, and sin when it is fully grown brings forth death." Temptation is sneaky—it wraps sin in attractive packaging, making rebellion feel justified. The enemy whispers lies that make us believe temporary satisfaction is worth the cost, all while leading us down a harmful path.

Then comes accusation, a mental and emotional attack that wears us down. Revelation 12:10 calls the enemy "the accuser of our brothers, who accuses them day and night before our God." These accusations aren't just reminders of our mistakes; they're heavy chains of guilt designed to drag us into despair. The enemy twists the concept of grace, focusing on our failures and burying our hope under layers of condemnation, trying to silence the voices meant to declare victory.

But the enemy's most dangerous tactic is deception. Jesus described him in John 8:44: "When he lies, he speaks out of his own character, for he is a liar and the father of lies." Deception blurs the lines between right and wrong, making it hard to distinguish truth from falsehood. It often hides in plain sight, camouflaged within our daily routines and justified by our emotions. It convinces us to chase desires that feel right but pull us away from what God truly intends for us.

Paul's story is a perfect example. Before his conversion, he genuinely believed he was fighting for righteousness by persecuting

Christians. His heart was sincere, but he was blinded by his own convictions. This shows how dangerous it can be to believe passionately in something that's completely wrong. The enemy thrives when we're confident but misguided.

Peter's journey highlights another tactic: emotional manipulation. Despite walking alongside Jesus, witnessing miracles firsthand, Peter denied knowing Him—out of sheer fear. This wasn't a logical decision; it was a panic response. The enemy uses our emotions against us, clouding our judgment and making us act out of impulse rather than truth.

In today's world, fear spreads like wildfire. Emotional reactions often override thoughtful reflection. We compromise our values for temporary comfort, becoming passionate about things that don't matter in the grand scheme. The enemy uses this emotional chaos to distract us from what truly counts.

Consider politics, for example. It's not inherently bad, but it can become a breeding ground for division. The enemy doesn't care which side you're on; he just wants you to forget your identity in Christ and replace it with

allegiance to an ideology. This can strain relationships—not over truth, but over differing
opinions. When we fight each other instead
of standing together, the enemy wins.

Words are another battleground. They carry immense power, capable of building up
or tearing down. In a world full of noise,
it's tempting to speak without thinking. But
wisdom often lies in thoughtful silence. Peter went from denying Jesus to boldly speaking the truth—not because he became a better speaker, but because his heart was transformed by the Holy Spirit.

Distraction is a subtle but effective tactic. It doesn't look harmful—just busy schedules, endless scrolling, or overwhelming to-do lists. But these things scatter our focus, slowly drifting us away from our connection with God. The enemy doesn't need us to fail spectacularly; a gradual drift is enough.

Paul's life after his conversion shows the power of focus. He didn't chase every opportunity; he pursued divine assignments. This kind of discernment comes from recognizing distraction as a tool the enemy uses to keep us from our purpose.

Knowledge is powerful, but it's not fool-proof. Even Satan used Scripture to tempt Jesus. The key is applying knowledge with wisdom and humility. This isn't about feeling ashamed of our struggles; it's about gaining clarity and strength to stand firm in our faith.

Shame isolates us, making us feel unworthy and alone. But God always reaches out, even when we pull away. Recognizing isolation as a tactic helps us seek connection and healing. Pride, another sneaky tactic, often masquerades as confidence but actually blocks growth. Paul had to confront his own pride before he could fully embrace God's grace.

Compromise creeps in quietly. Peter compromised under pressure, denying Jesus. Small concessions can slowly erode our faith. Comparison is another joy-stealer. The enemy uses it to breed discontentment, but focusing on our unique paths helps us find peace.

Doubt isn't a sign of failure; it's a crossroads. The enemy uses doubt to delay our obedience to God. Offense, too, can divide us if we're not careful. Jesus and Paul faced countless offenses, but they chose forgiveness and unity.

Control feels like security, but it often stems from fear. Paul learned to find strength in surrender, trusting God instead of holding on tightly. Jesus Himself showed us how to stay clear-headed amid confusion. He responded to temptation with truth, stayed emotionally grounded, and focused on His mission.

Our children face these battles early, too. Teaching them to recognize the enemy's tactics—like distraction, shame, pride, isolation, compromise, comparison, doubt, offense, and control—prepares them to stand strong. When we model truth, grace, emotional discipline, and a deep connection with

God, we equip the next generation to grow not just in belief but in lasting spiritual strength.

Mastering our emotions isn't about suppressing them; it's about ensuring they don't control us. Emotions, while natural and God-given, can be manipulated when left unchecked. The enemy thrives on emotional chaos, using fear, anger, pride, and even misplaced passion to cloud our judgment. Recognizing this helps us pause, reflect, and respond thoughtfully rather than react impulsively. By anchoring ourselves in truth and maintaining emotional discipline, we guard our hearts against deception and maintain clarity in spiritual battles.

Equally vital is our ability to discern the tactics used against us. Awareness is the first line of defense. When we understand how fear isolates, how temptation disguises itself, and how deception blurs truth, we're better equipped to stand firm. This isn't just intellectual knowledge—it's spiritual vigilance. By staying rooted in God's Word, connected through prayer, and supported by community, we sharpen our discernment. This awareness, combined with emotional resilience, transforms us from vulnerable targets into steadfast warriors, capable of living with purpose and conviction.

CHAPTER 7

JESUS NAME

W hen you hear the name of Jesus, what comes to mind? It's more than just a name—it holds profound meaning, embodying salvation, authority, and the very presence of the divine. As we explore this together, let's reflect on the truths Scripture reveals about the power behind His name.

Consider Acts 4:12, where it says, "And there is salvation in no one else, for there is no other name under heaven given among men by which we must be saved." This isn't just a statement; it's the cornerstone of our faith. The name of Jesus isn't a mere label—it's the exclusive pathway to redemption, anchoring our hope and trust in Him alone. When we say His name, we're declaring our reliance on the one true source of salvation.

Paul echoes this sentiment in Philippians 2:9-11: "Therefore God has highly exalted him and bestowed on him the name that is above every name, so that at the name of Jesus every knee should bow, in heaven and on earth and under the earth, and every tongue confess that Jesus Christ is Lord, to the glory of God the Father." Imagine that—every knee, every tongue, across all of creation, acknowledging His supreme authority. His name bridges heaven and earth, touching both the present and the eternal.

But His name isn't just about distant reverence—it holds power right here and now. The name of Jesus brings hope where there's despair, light where darkness tries to creep in, and life where things feel broken. His miracles aren't confined to ancient texts; they're alive in the stories and experiences of countless believers today.

I've always been captivated by the accounts of Jesus confronting demon-possessed individuals. What's striking is that these dark forces didn't need an introduction. They recognized Him instantly—Jesus, the Son of God. No hesitation, no confusion. Their immediate acknowledgment of His authority is staggering, especially when you realize even His closest followers were still grappling with His true identity. That contrast speaks volumes about His unmatched power. Even forces of darkness had no choice but to submit to Him.

Now, let's think about His miracles. Healing the blind, raising the dead, calming storms, feeding thousands—these weren't just displays of divine power. They were acts of deep compassion intertwined with absolute authority. When Jesus spoke, nature listened. Sickness vanished. Demons fled. His words carried life, healing, and restoration. And here's the incredible part: that same power is alive in His name today.

I've witnessed this firsthand during my time working in the emergency room. There was a patient—no signs of life after an intense, hour-long code. We did everything we could, but eventually, the family agreed to call the time of death. As we were preparing the patient for the family, she suddenly sat up, looked around, and asked, "Where am I?" In that sterile, chaotic room, we experienced something no medical explanation could cover. That was Jesus. His power broke through, defying every expectation.

Another moment etched in my heart was during my senior year of high school. I was at football practice when my dad rushed in, panic-stricken, shouting that my mom had been in a terrible accident. The doctors described her survival as nothing short of miraculous. She faced several severe accidents over time, and each recovery left medical professionals baffled. Each time, I saw the undeniable mark of Jesus' intervention.

But His name isn't just about physical miracles. It brings peace in the most profound emotional pain. I remember having three close friends growing up. We shared everything, and our last beach trip together is a memory I cherish deeply. Life took us in different directions, and those friendships faded. Grieving friendships is unique—the people are still out there, but the connection is gone. Yet, Jesus helps us carry these people in our hearts, love them from afar, and find peace in the memories. His name bridges the gap between our sorrows and His comfort.

When life feels overwhelming—grief, anxiety, despair—just whispering His name can calm the storm within. His name is a refuge, a strong tower where the weary find rest. He offers peace that surpasses all understanding, grounding us when everything feels unsteady.

Prayer is powerful. It's not just a passive ritual; it's our direct line to Jesus. Some might dismiss it with a casual, "Oh, just pray about it," as if it's insignificant. But prayer isn't a last resort. It's our first defense, our strongest weapon. When we pray, we're invoking the name above all names, engaging with the One who holds the universe in His hands. Every prayer shifts something—whether in us, around us, or in ways we may never fully understand.

Even in today's skeptical world, the power of Jesus' name remains unmatched. People might mock it, dismiss it, or doubt it, but His name continues to heal, restore, and transform lives. For those who've experienced His touch, there's no question. His name has brought life where death seemed certain, peace in chaos, and healing beyond comprehension.

This isn't about religious rituals or perfect words. It's about calling on the One who conquered death. Every breath we take testifies to His sustaining power. Every sunrise reminds us of His faithfulness. His miracles, both big and small, shout His name through creation, showing us His continuous work in our lives.

So, when you face insurmountable odds, remember the woman who sat up after being declared dead, my mother's miraculous recoveries, and the peace found even in lost friendships. Each story is a testament to Jesus' enduring presence and power.

There's no secret formula. It's simply Jesus. His name carries authority in heaven and on earth. His name is our hope, our peace, our salvation. When life feels too heavy, when grief overwhelms, when doubt creeps in—speak His name. Jesus.

In His name, we find everything we need.

He's the same yesterday, today, and forever. His power hasn't faded with time or culture. No matter who doubts, the truth remains: There is power in the name of Jesus.

Call on Him. Trust in Him. You'll witness His power at work in your life, just like I have.

Jesus. That's all it takes.

CHAPTER 8

GOD'S VOICE

Y ou know, the voice of God isn't some distant, faint echo that we have to strain to hear. It's more like a roaring presence that cuts right through all the noise and distractions of our lives. Think about Hebrews 4:12, where it says, "For the word of God is living and active, sharper than any two-edged sword, piercing to the division of soul and of spirit, of joints and of marrow, and discerning the thoughts and intentions of the heart." God's voice doesn't just talk at us—it penetrates deep within, slicing through the layers of our hearts to reveal the truth, even the parts we try to keep hidden. In the chaos of life, His word stands tall and unwavering, like a lighthouse guiding us through a storm, demanding not just to be heard but to be responded to.

When God speaks, it's not just a simple message; it's cosmic. The heavens, the earth—everything listens. Psalm 29:4–5 paints this vivid picture: "The voice of the Lord is powerful; the voice of the Lord is full of majesty. The voice of the Lord breaks the cedars; the Lord breaks the cedars of Lebanon." Imagine that—His voice has the power to shatter the mightiest trees, dismantle strongholds of fear and doubt, and break down the barriers we think are unmovable. It's not a timid whisper but a thunderous call that stirs the soul, awakens our hearts, and demands that we step out of our comfort zones and into the full force of His divine plan.

But here's the beautiful thing—God's voice isn't always loud and booming. Sometimes, it's a soft whisper, tucked away in the quiet moments of our hearts. It's transformative, whether it's shaking the ground beneath us or gently nudging us when we least expect it. To really hear God, we've got to tune in, like adjusting a radio to get the perfect signal. It's about being open, sensitive, and still, learning to recognize His voice amid life's constant background noise. His words bring wisdom that goes beyond logic, comfort when everything feels dark, and correction when we're veering off track. His voice doesn't just speak to us—it reaches into the depths of who we are, beyond culture, language, and circumstance, rooted in the eternal and unchanging nature of God Himself.

So, how do we get better at hearing Him? It starts with intentional stillness. Sounds simple, right? But in today's world, where we're constantly bombarded with notifications, deadlines, and distractions, creating pockets of silence feels almost revolutionary. Through prayer, quiet reflection, and immersing ourselves in Scripture, we carve out sacred spaces where God's voice can rise above the noise. And His voice? It's not confined to one way of speaking. It might come as an overwhelming sense of peace, a strong inner conviction, or even through the words of a friend, a song, or the beauty of the natural world around us.

The incredible part is that God's voice isn't limited to church pews or quiet mornings. He speaks in the everyday, in the mundane, and in the miraculous. Whether you're savoring a peaceful sunrise, navigating a hectic work-day, or wrestling with life's biggest questions, His voice is there—accessible, clear, and con-stant. Often, it's in our most vulnerable mo-ments, when we feel exposed and raw, that

His words of comfort and guidance resonate the loudest. But even in seasons of joy and abundance, He's there, celebrating with us and reminding us that His love and presence are unwavering.

Why does God speak to us? Because He wants a relationship, not just a checklist of good deeds or religious routines. Unlike distant, impersonal deities from ancient myths, the Creator of the universe longs for intimacy with us. His voice reassures us of who we are, provides direction when we're lost, and anchors us in truth when life feels shaky. It's personal—it's about connection, love, and walking through life hand-in-hand with the One who knows us best.

And if you have kids, teaching them to listen for God's voice is one of the greatest gifts you can give. It's more than just passing on religious traditions; it's about giving them a compass that never fails. The world tosses out fleeting trends and shifting values, but God's voice offers eternal truths, unconditional love, and guidance rooted in righteousness. When children learn to recognize His voice early, they build a resilience that helps them stand firm, even when peer pressure and societal expectations try to pull them in different directions.

This foundation becomes their anchor. They learn that their worth doesn't come from likes on social media or the approval of others, but from the unchanging love of God. It gives them clarity when they face tough decisions and confidence to stand firm in their faith. In a world eager to shape their hearts and minds, God's voice becomes the steady, guiding light they can always rely on.

Now, God's voice isn't just for the tough times. Sure, when we're hurting, His words can be like a balm for our souls, piercing through the darkness with hope and peace. But He also speaks in the good times—in our successes, celebrations, and victories. His voice calls us to gratitude, keeps us humble, and reminds us not to get too comfortable or self-reliant. It's a gentle nudge that says, "Hey, don't forget who's walking this journey with you." That ongoing dialogue deepens our relationship with Him, helping us grow and stay grounded no matter what life throws our way.

Sometimes, though, we struggle to hear Him. We expect burning bushes and dramatic revelations, but often, God speaks through the ordinary—a friend's kind words, a song lyric that hits just right, or a sudden moment of clarity. It takes practice and spiritual discernment to recognize these moments. It's like learning to pick out a loved one's voice in a crowded room—familiarity makes it easier to recognize.

Distractions can be big roadblocks, too. The constant buzz of media, responsibilities, and life's chaos can drown out the whispers of God. That's why carving out quiet time is so important. Whether through journaling, worship, or just sitting in silence, these practices help us center ourselves and create space where God's voice can break through.

Doubt can sneak in as well. We wonder, "Is this really God, or just my own thoughts?" That's where Scripture comes in handy. God's voice will never contradict His Word. It's always loving, just, merciful, and true. Talking with trusted, mature believers can also help confirm what we're hearing. Prayer, patience, and wise counsel are key tools for clarity.

Above all, trust is foundational. Believing that God wants to speak to you—that He desires that connection—opens your heart to hear Him more clearly. You don't need to be a spiritual superstar to hear His voice. It's not reserved for pastors or prophets. It's for everyone who seeks Him with a genuine heart. That assurance takes the pressure off and invites us into a real, authentic relationship with Him.

When God speaks, His voice brings conviction, not condemnation. It points out areas where we need to grow, but it's always rooted in love. Unlike the enemy's voice, which shames and accuses, God's voice is filled with hope and the desire for our best. Even when it's challenging, it draws us closer to Him, shaping us into who we're meant to be.

There will be seasons when hearing His voice feels like trudging through a spiritual desert. These "wilderness" times aren't signs that God has abandoned us. They're opportunities to deepen our trust, to lean on His promises even when we don't feel His presence. Staying connected through prayer and Scripture during these dry spells builds spiritual muscles. And often, when we look back, we realize He was there all along, working behind the scenes.

Gratitude plays a huge role in tuning into God's voice. When we cultivate a thankful heart, we become more aware of His presence in the little things—a child's laughter, a stunning sunset, a random act of kindness. This awareness blurs the line between sacred and ordinary, turning every moment into a chance to connect with Him.

Ultimately, hearing God's voice isn't just about personal growth. It's about living out our purpose. His guidance gives us clarity, courage, and confirmation. It transforms everyday tasks into sacred missions with eternal impact. And when we model this for our children—sharing our experiences, praying openly, and seeking God's direction—they see faith in action. It becomes real, tangible, and inspiring.

God's voice doesn't just speak to us; it moves us to act with love, compassion, and kindness. It's not just about what we receive but how we respond—serving others, encouraging those around us, and reflecting His grace. Listening to His voice is life-changing, not just for us but for everyone we encounter.

At the end of the day, the voice of God is our anchor. It grounds us in truth, offers hope, and lights our path. Whether through Scripture, prayer, life's twists and turns, or quiet whispers in our hearts, His voice remains con-

stant and trustworthy. Embracing this divine dialogue doesn't just transform our lives—it has the power to change the world around us.

CHAPTER 9

FEAR NOT

You know, fear in the scriptures isn't just some distant, abstract idea. It's real. It's raw. It's that gut-wrenching, heart-racing force that grips both saints and sinners alike. Take David, for instance. In Psalm 55:5, he doesn't sugarcoat it. He cries out, "Fear and

trembling come upon me, and horror overwhelms me." Can you feel that? His words
drip with emotion, like someone cornered
with nowhere to run. This isn't the kind of
fear you can ignore or push aside. It's the type
that invades your soul, shaking the very foundation of your faith, making your knees weak
and your heart pound. It strips away the illusion of control, forcing you to face what's
lurking inside and what's beyond your understanding.

Now, picture the disciples caught in that
terrifying storm on the Sea of Galilee. The
waves are roaring, the boat's lurching like it's

about to be swallowed whole, and there's Jesus—calm, unshaken. In Mark 4:40, He rebukes them, "Why are you so afraid? Have you still no faith?" Their fear wasn't baseless. The danger was real. But here's the kicker—it wasn't just the storm outside that terrified them. It was the storm within. Their panic revealed the cracks in their trust, the struggle to believe even when the Savior Himself was right there with them. Fear became a mirror, reflecting not just the danger but their doubts, their fragile faith. It's in these moments that faith isn't just tested—it's exposed.

And then there's Jesus in the Garden of Gethsemane. This is where it gets deeply personal. Luke 22:44 paints the scene vividly: "And being in agony, He prayed more earnestly; and His sweat became like great drops of blood falling down to the ground." Imagine that. The Son of God, wrestling with overwhelming fear. This wasn't a sign of weakness. It was the weight of divine purpose colliding with human vulnerability. His fear was intense, suffocating even, but within that crucible of dread, perfect obedience was forged. He didn't pray to escape the fear. He prayed for the strength to endure it. That's courage—not the absence of fear, but standing firm in spite of it.

But here's the good news: the Bible doesn't leave us stranded in our fear. Isaiah 41:10 isn't a gentle pat on the back; it's a bold declaration, "Fear not, for I am with you; be not dismayed, for I am your God." This isn't a comforting suggestion—it's a command, a lifeline tossed into the turbulent waters. Fear may roar like a flood, but God's presence is the rock that doesn't move. The scriptures don't dismiss fear; they confront it head-on. They don't downplay it; they magnify the power of the One who stands above it. In your darkest moments, when fear feels overwhelming, remember this: fear is real, but so is the God who reigns over it.

Let's be honest—fear and doubt aren't just words we throw around. They're forces that grip us, twisting our hearts, clouding our minds. They sneak in uninvited, turning peaceful moments into storms of anxiety. They expose our fragile humanity, highlighting vulnerabilities we'd rather ignore. But here's the twist: these emotions aren't signs of failure. They are the battlegrounds where courage is born.

Every single day, fear and doubt show up like uninvited guests. They don't knock; they burst through the door. I face them. You face them. Even Jesus faced them.

His disciples? They didn't get it. They had front-row seats to His miracles, yet stumbled over disbelief. He told them plainly about His death and resurrection, but fear made it hard to comprehend. Let's be real—if someone told you that your brutal death was around the corner, would you walk into it willingly? I wouldn't. Fear paralyzes. Doubt blinds.

Then there's Judas. Maybe it was greed, maybe fear, or a twisted mix of both that drove him to betray Jesus with a kiss—a symbol of love turned into an act of treachery. But that was just the beginning. The whip sang its cruel song against Jesus' back, each strike a painful symphony of suffering. Blood mixed with dust. The crowd's roars drowned out any shred of mercy. The cross wasn't just wood; it was the crushing weight of humanity's sins splintering into His flesh.

On that cross, breath ragged, Jesus cried out, "My God, My God, why have You forsaken Me?" Not a cry of defeat, but a declaration, a fulfillment of prophecy. Psalm 22 echoed through the darkness, His agony wrapped in scripture, His suffering pointing us back to God's plan.

And here's the heart of it all: even in the abyss of pain, Jesus held on—not to life, but to purpose. His love didn't shatter under the weight of fear. It burned brighter. He endured, not because He was fearless, but because His love was greater than His fear.

Isn't it fascinating how fear works? It grips us, twists our hearts, and clouds our minds, yet Jesus faced it head-on. He knew every painful detail—the betrayal, the beatings, the cross. He understood the agony waiting for Him, and still, He chose it. Think about that.

Despite knowing the end result, despite the suffocating fear in Gethsemane, He didn't back down. Why? So we wouldn't have to carry that weight ourselves. His love outmatched His fear. He faced the cross with full knowledge of its horror because His purpose was greater than His pain—and that purpose was you and me.

That's the gospel. Jesus didn't just die; He conquered. Fear and death thought they'd won. But three days later, the stone was rolled away, and the tomb stood empty. Victory didn't come with armies or swords. It came with scars and resurrection.

Fear and doubt? They're part of life. But they're not unbeatable. Jesus showed us that. He didn't avoid them. He faced them, crushed them with faith and purpose. And so can we.

The story doesn't end at the cross. It doesn't end at the tomb. It doesn't end. The battle continues—in me, in you. So turn the page. Face your fears. The fight isn't over.

And if you forget everything else, remember this: the most repeated command in the Bible is "Fear not." Not because fear isn't real, but because God is with you. Always.

CHAPTER 10

PRAYER

"The prayer of a righteous person has great power as it is working."
—James 5:16 (ESV)

Have you ever thought about how powerful prayer really is? It's not just words floating into the air, hoping to land somewhere meaningful. No, prayer is this dynamic force, alive with purpose and power. Imagine the heavens standing still, the earth holding its breath when the heartfelt cry of a believer pierces through the divide between the seen and unseen. That's what prayer does—it shakes things up in ways we can't always see but can definitely feel.

Take Elijah, for example. He was just like us, a regular person with struggles, doubts, and fears. Yet when he prayed earnestly that it wouldn't rain, the skies listened. For three and a half years, not a drop fell. Then he prayed again, and the heavens responded with abundance (James 5:17-18). Isn't that incredible? It shows that prayer isn't about being perfect; it's about being persistent, bold, and full of faith. It's like wielding a spiritual weapon that can tear down strongholds and summon God's power right into the middle of our human struggles.

When we pray, we're not approaching God as beggars hoping for scraps. We come as warriors clothed in righteousness. Our prayers echo in the courts of heaven, not as faint whispers but as declarations of faith. Think about Jesus in the Garden of Gethsemane. He wasn't just casually talking to God.

He prayed so fervently that His sweat became like drops of blood (Luke 22:44). His prayers weren't passive; they were battles, waged in the depths of His spirit, aligning His heart with God's will even in the face of unimaginable suffering.

Prayer is more than a routine or a checkbox on our spiritual to-do list. It's the very heartbeat of our relationship with God. Jesus said in Matthew 6:6, "But when you pray, go into your room, close the door and pray to your Father, who is unseen. Then your Father, who sees what is done in secret, will reward you." This isn't just about finding a quiet space. It's about creating a sacred encounter where authenticity thrives, where we can be real with God without pretense or performance.

You know, I've found that making prayer a regular part of my day has transformed my spiritual life. It's not out of obligation but because it's become a cherished appointment with God. Life gets busy, distractions pile up, but when I treat prayer as non-negotiable, it shifts from being an afterthought to a foundational practice. Some days, my prayers feel rushed or distracted, but even in those imperfect moments, there's a closeness with God that grows deeper over time.

And here's the beautiful part—prayer isn't about having the right words. Romans 8:26 reminds us, "In the same way, the Spirit helps us in our weakness. We do not know what we ought to pray for, but the Spirit himself intercedes for us through wordless groans." Isn't that freeing? Even when we don't know what to say, the Holy Spirit steps in, translating our hearts' cries into heavenly language. It's not about perfection; it's about presence.

Consistent prayer builds spiritual resilience. Think of it like exercising a muscle—the more you do it, the stronger you become. 1 Thessalonians 5:17 tells us to "pray without ceasing." That doesn't mean we're on our knees 24/7, but it does mean weaving prayer into every part of our lives. Whether we're celebrating, struggling, or just going through the motions of a regular day, prayer keeps us connected to God's presence.

Through prayer, we not only speak but learn to listen. Jeremiah 33:3 says, "Call to me and I will answer you and tell you great and unsearchable things you do not know." Prayer shifts from being a monologue to a dialogue. It's a space where we pour out our hearts and also pause to hear God's voice, gaining wisdom and clarity we couldn't find on our own.

I've realized that even my most imperfect prayers are precious to God. There's beauty in showing up, even when I'm distracted or doubting. The psalmists did it all the time—crying out with raw honesty. Psalm 62:8 encourages us, "Trust in him at all times, you people; pour out your hearts to him, for God is our refuge." God isn't looking for polished words; He's looking for honest hearts.

So, at the end of the day, prayer isn't just an activity. It's the heartbeat of our faith. It's where battles are fought, peace is found, and hearts are transformed. Whether your prayers are long or short, eloquent or messy, what matters is showing up, day after day, letting prayer shape and strengthen your life.

CHAPTER 11

THE POWER OF SCRIPTURE

Imagine sitting across from a friend, deeply engaged in a heartfelt conversation about the power of Scripture. You lean in and say, "You know, the word of God isn't just ink on pages. It's alive, active, and sharper than any double-edged sword. It cuts right through to the core—dividing soul and spirit, even piercing joints and marrow. It discerns the thoughts and intentions buried deep within our hearts." That's straight out of Hebrews 4:12, and it's not just poetic language. The Scriptures aren't dormant relics tucked away on ancient scrolls—they're alive, brimming with power that slices through pretense and exposes the truth within us.

Think about it: neglecting God's word is like stepping onto a battlefield without armor. Life throws subtle deceptions our way, and without Scripture, we're defenseless. The Bible isn't meant to sit quietly on a shelf; it demands our attention, inviting us to not just read but to dive deep, understand, and let it transform us from the inside out.

Then there's this powerful reminder in 2 Timothy 3:16-17: "All Scripture is breathed out by God and profitable for teaching, for reproof, for correction, and for training in righteousness." This isn't just a casual suggestion—it's a divine directive. Scripture is God's very breath, designed to guide, correct, and prepare us for the challenges of righteous living. Without it, we're like sailors adrift without an anchor, vulnerable to the shifting tides of life.

Have you ever thought of Scripture as a treasure? It's more than an ancient collection of texts; it's the living, breathing Word of God, pulsating with divine wisdom and unshakable guidance. It breathes life into weary souls, ignites hearts with truth, and anchors us firmly in God's eternal promises. In a world swirling with conflicting ideologies, the Bible stands tall—a beacon of clarity and truth.

Jesus Himself said, "Sanctify them by the truth; Your word is truth" (John 17:17). Knowing Scripture helps us discern truth from lies, anchoring us amidst life's chaos. Each verse becomes a lens through which we evaluate every claim and philosophy, protecting us from subtle deceptions that aim to lead us astray.

And here's the thing—Scripture isn't just a source of knowledge; it's a weapon. Paul tells us in Ephesians 6:17 to "Take the helmet of salvation and the sword of the Spirit, which is the word of God." Picture it: standing on a battlefield, armed with a sword that cuts through lies, temptation, and the enemy's schemes. Without it, we're vulnerable, but with it, we stand bold and unshaken.

Even Satan knows the power of Scripture. Remember when he tempted Jesus in the wilderness? He twisted Scripture, trying to deceive the Son of God. But Jesus countered every lie with accurate, contextually sound Scripture. His response wasn't passive; it was a forceful declaration of truth, showing us the importance of not just knowing the Word but grasping its depth and divine intent.

Through Scripture, God reveals His character—His justice, mercy, love, and unwavering commitment to truth. Psalm 119:105 beautifully captures this: "Your word is a lamp to my feet and a light for my path." It illuminates our way, guiding us with compassionate truth amidst life's darkness.

Scripture isn't just for guidance; it's God's chosen tool to defeat evil. Jesus didn't need physical might to overcome Satan—He declared Scripture with authority. This speaks to a timeless truth: the enemy cannot withstand the authority of God's Word when we wield it with unwavering faith.

Prophecies fulfilled through Christ's life, death, and resurrection showcase Scripture's reliability and divine orchestration. As Jesus said in Matthew 5:17, "I have not come to abolish the Law or the Prophets but to fulfill them." His life wasn't just a story; it was prophecy fulfilled with divine precision.

The knowledge of Scripture builds resilience, nurturing faith like deep roots, strengthening hope, and deepening love. When trials come, it's the Word hidden in our hearts that anchors us. Psalm 119:11 says it best: "I have hidden Your word in my heart that I might not sin against You."

Scripture's transformative power is undeniable. It pierces through superficial layers, exposing hidden wounds, correcting distorted thinking, and healing brokenness. Through it, the Holy Spirit convicts us, reveals God's grace, and shapes us into Christ's image.

For believers, knowing Scripture isn't optional—it's vital. It's our defense, our compass, our sword, and the revelation of God's heart. To stand firm in faith, resist the enemy, and live with purpose, we must immerse ourselves in His Word. Let it dwell richly within us, guiding our actions and shaping our identity.

So dive into Scripture—not as an obligation but as a lifeline. Let its words thunder in your soul, ignite your spirit, and anchor your heart. This is no ordinary book—it's the voice of God, calling, equipping, and transforming. Embrace it, wield it, live it—and watch how it shapes not just your life but the world around you.

CHAPTER 12

BORN TO STAND OUT

H ave you ever wondered what it really means to stand out? I mean, do we actually strive for this in our daily lives? If we're honest, most of us prefer to blend in, right? It feels safer that way, more comfortable. But here's the thing—Jesus actually warned us about this tendency. Knowing that, why do we still do it? Maybe because fitting in feels like the path of least resistance. But is that the path we're meant to walk?

Let's dive into Romans 12:2. It says, "Do not be conformed to this world, but be transformed by the renewal of your mind, that by testing you may discern what is the will of God, what is good and acceptable and perfect." That's not just a gentle nudge; it's a clear, bold command. It's like God is saying, "Hey, don't let the world squeeze you into its mold." The world tries hard to reshape us, pushing ideas that often stray far from

God's heart. But we're called to resist that pressure actively. This isn't a passive transformation—it's a daily choice to stand firm, to renew our minds and align our hearts with Christ.

Now, think about 1 John 2:15-17: "Do not love the world or the things in the world. If anyone loves the world, the love of the Father is not in him." That hits hard, doesn't it? It's impossible to give our hearts fully to both God and the world. The world offers fleeting pleasures, quick fixes that don't last. But life with Christ? That's where true, eternal joy is found. When we live set apart, our lives should make people pause. They should see a difference—a light shining so brightly it stirs curiosity, maybe even discomfort, because it's a light that darkness can't understand.

Then there's Galatians 1:10: "For am I now seeking the approval of man, or of God? Or am I trying to please man? If I were still trying to please man, I would not be a servant of Christ." Ouch. That really calls us out, doesn't it? Chasing human approval is a trap. It keeps us from living boldly for Christ. As His followers, we're not here to blend in; we're here to reflect His character. And that takes guts—courage to stand tall when it feels like the world is against you.

We weren't created to live small, safe lives. We were born to ignite, to burn brightly with the fire of Jesus within us. Each of us has a purpose crafted by God Himself, a purpose that echoes through eternity. This isn't about making our names great—it's about making His name known. Jesus didn't fit in. He challenged norms, defied expectations, and lived with radical obedience to the Father. His life was a bold declaration to stand out, no matter the cost.

Standing out means loving in ways the world doesn't understand. It's loving fiercely, forgiving freely—even when it's hard. It's choosing grace over grudges and compassion over judgment. Jesus didn't just talk about love; He lived it. Every action, every word, was love in motion.

And forgiveness? It's not optional. It's revolutionary. Jesus forgave the very people who nailed Him to the cross. So, what's holding us back? Holding onto anger and resentment only hurts us. Forgiveness sets us free.

Truth isn't up for debate. It's sharp, powerful, and sometimes uncomfortable. Jesus spoke the truth boldly, even when it cost Him everything. Today, speaking biblical truth might cost us relationships, opportunities, or popularity. But we weren't called to be popular—we were called to be light in the darkness.

The Great Commission isn't a casual suggestion; it's our mission. "Go. Make disciples." That means stepping out of our comfort zones, sharing our faith, and living it out loud. Our stories, struggles, and scars are powerful tools God uses to reach others.

Your past mistakes? They don't disqualify you. They're part of your testimony. God takes our failures and turns them into stories of redemption. You're not defined by your past—you're defined by His grace.

It's easy to talk about faith, but living it out is where the real challenge lies. Actions speak louder than words. When people see the transformation in your life, they'll notice. They might question your beliefs, but they can't deny the change they see.

Words matter too. Speak the truth boldly, but always wrap it in love. The Gospel is both powerful and tender, convicting and comforting. It's a balance of grace and truth.

Standing out often means standing alone. But you're in good company—think of Daniel, Esther, Paul. Their courage changed history. Yours can too.

Worried about being "canceled" or rejected? That's okay. It means you're making waves. But remember, your worth isn't in others' approval—it's rooted in Christ.

Authenticity is powerful. The world doesn't need more perfect facades; it needs real, raw faith. Share your struggles. Show your scars. Let people see Jesus in your mess because that's where His grace shines the brightest.

You're not meant to do this alone. Community is essential. Surround yourself with people who encourage, challenge, and pray with you. They'll remind you who you are when the world tries to make you forget.

Prayer isn't just a quiet ritual; it's spiritual warfare. It changes things. When fear creeps in, pray louder. When doubt whispers, hit your knees and fight back with faith.

Jesus never promised an easy life. But He promised victory. Challenges are part of the journey, but take heart—He's already overcome the world. And because of that, so will you.

Obedience will cost you. It might cost comfort, convenience, even relationships. But the reward? A life with eternal impact. A legacy that points people to Jesus.

Shift your focus. Temporary struggles are nothing compared to eternal glory. We're not living for applause—we're living for that moment when we hear, "Well done, good and faithful servant."

Joy isn't based on circumstances. It's rooted in Christ. It's praising through pain, dancing in the storms, and smiling through tears because your hope isn't in this world—it's in Him.

Grace isn't a crutch; it's fuel. You'll stumble, but grace picks you up and keeps you going. Boldness doesn't come from personality; it's birthed from knowing God deeply.

When people look at your life, let them see Jesus. Not in perfection, but in perseverance. In grace, love, and truth. Live boldly. Love fiercely. Stand unapologetically for Christ.

Humility keeps us grounded. We're not the heroes—Jesus is. We're just vessels, imperfect but filled with divine purpose.

Hope isn't wishful thinking; it's an anchor. Strong, secure, and unwavering. In a world drowning in despair, your hope shines like a beacon.

The Holy Spirit isn't just an accessory; He's our source of power and guidance. We're not called to survive—we're called to thrive.

Legacy isn't about what you leave behind; it's about who you impact. Your faith can inspire generations.

Why stand out? Because Jesus stood in your place. He bore your sins, faced rejection, and conquered death for you. Now it's your turn. Stand out. Stand firm. Stand for Him.

This isn't just a message—it's a challenge. Are you ready?

CHAPTER 13

CHILDLIKE PERSISTENCE

"Ask, and it will be given to you; seek, and you will find; knock, and it will be opened to you." — Matthew 7:7 (ESV)

You ever notice how kids just keep asking for what they want? They don't hold back. They'll tug at your sleeve, repeat the same question a dozen times, and they don't worry about sounding annoying. They're relentless. That's exactly the kind of persistence Jesus talks about when He invites us to come to Him. He's not looking for perfectly phrased prayers or polished words. He wants hearts that won't give up, hearts that knock on Heaven's door with the determination of a child who refuses to be ignored.

Take the Canaanite woman in Matthew 15:22-28. She cried out, "Have mercy on me, O Lord, Son of David; my daughter is severely oppressed by a demon." Jesus didn't answer right away. The disciples wanted to send her away. But she didn't stop. She got closer, dropped to her knees, and pleaded, "Lord, help me." Even when Jesus tested her with a challenging response, she stood firm. And you know what He said? "O woman, great is your faith!" Her persistence moved Him to act.

So, why does God honor persistence like that? Because it shows how much we believe. It reveals hearts that won't settle for less than God's presence. Remember the story in Luke 18:1-8 about the persistent widow? She kept coming to an unjust judge, asking for justice. He didn't care about God or people, but her persistence wore him down. Jesus points out, "And will not God give justice to His elect, who cry to Him day and night?" It's not about being noisy—it's about having relentless faith.

Prayer isn't just a polite, one-time thing. It's spiritual warfare. It's laying siege to Heaven's gates until they open wide. Matthew 11:12 says, "The kingdom of heaven has suffered violence, and the violent take it by force." This isn't passive faith. It's bold, fierce, and stubborn in hope.

Think about it—kids don't overthink it. They ask shamelessly, seek tirelessly, and knock like their life depends on it. And what's the promise? "For everyone who asks receives, and the one who seeks finds, and to the one who knocks it will be opened" (Matthew 7:8).

We admire persistence in others—people who don't give up, who keep going despite setbacks. But when it's our turn, we hesitate. We fear rejection. We get tired. Kids don't have that problem. They're naturally curious and full of hope. They don't need pep talks—they just believe. Rejection doesn't faze them. A "no" today doesn't mean "no" forever. They'll ask again, minutes later, as if they've never heard the word "no."

Picture your five-year-old asking, "Are the Power Rangers real? Can they come to my birthday party?" over and over, eyes bright with excitement. Each time they ask, it's like a new chance for a different answer. They're not being redundant—they're hopeful. Their persistence is fueled by belief.

Adults, though? We lose that spark. We become cautious, worried about what others think, afraid of failure. But what if we got that boldness back? What if we chased our dreams and prayed with the same fearless intensity as a child?

Imagine your three-year-old asking, "Can I be a real mermaid? Can I have ice cream and Skittles for breakfast?" a thousand times, each request filled with hope, undeterred by denial. They don't focus on what's impossible—they focus on what they want.

Kids have laser focus. They don't get stuck in "what ifs." Their minds aren't cluttered with doubt. Their hearts are all in. That kind of focus fuels their persistence and relentless optimism.

Now, what if we prayed like that? What if we approached God with that same fire, stripping away doubt and fear? In Luke 18, Jesus tells about the persistent widow again. She kept pleading with the unjust judge until he gave in—not because he cared, but because she wore him out. If persistence can move an indifferent judge, imagine what it does with our loving, compassionate Father.

God loves our repeated prayers. He doesn't get tired of hearing us ask. In fact, He delights in it. Our persistence shows our dependence on Him. It's not a sign of weak faith—it's proof of steadfast trust. Every time we pray, we're declaring, "I believe You're listening."

God's patience is endless. No busy signals. No locked doors. No "do not disturb" signs. His heart is always open. His ears are always tuned in. Every prayer strengthens our faith, shapes our character, and deepens our trust.

Kids show us how to ask without fear. They don't let a "no" define them. Hope anchors their hearts. As adults, we can reclaim that courage.

Childlike persistence isn't just endearing—it's powerful. It's the key to a faith walk that doesn't quit, even when answers seem delayed or distant. Jesus invites us to approach Him with that same unrelenting spirit, not because He needs to be convinced, but because it changes us. Every time we ask, seek, and knock with the fierce hope of a child, we're declaring our trust in His goodness. We're reminding our hearts that He is listening, that He cares, and that He answers in His perfect timing. So don't hold back. Pray boldly. Keep knocking. Let your faith be as stubborn as a child's hope—undaunted, relentless, and full of expectation.

CHAPTER 14

BREAKDOWN BEFORE BREAKTHROUGH

You know, life has this brutal way of tossing us into the deep end, doesn't it? When despair grips you so tight it feels like you can't breathe, and hope is just a flicker barely holding on—that's when the soul screams its rawest, truest cry. Think about Mary Magdalene. She wasn't just some woman with a complicated past; she was battling seven demons, each one leaving scars on her spirit, dragging her deeper into darkness. But even under all that wreckage, her heart was burning, fiercely hungry for something more—for redemption.

Then came Jesus. One encounter with Him, and everything shifted. Imagine her world—broken, messy, hopeless—suddenly exploding with light and possibility. At the cross, as she stood there shattered, her sobs weren't just silent tears; they ripped through the heavy, suffocating silence, mixing with desperate prayers. But here's the thing—her agony didn't drown her. No, it was like a spark that ignited a spiritual awakening. She wasn't just there to witness the resurrection; she was the very first, standing right at the edge where history itself was reborn.

And then there's Paul. You probably know he was Saul first—a man fueled by relentless ambition, hunting down Christians with this fierce, blinding zeal. But then Damascus happened. A blinding light, a voice that thundered through his soul, and suddenly, darkness swallowed him whole. His pride? Shattered like fragile glass underfoot. He was left blind, broken, powerless. And that's exactly where God did His work—not in Saul's strength but in his ruin. From those ashes rose Paul, an apostle whose words still set hearts on fire centuries later.

Here's a hard truth: breakdowns aren't just random accidents. They're divine detonations. They blow apart the illusions we cling to, strip away the masks we wear, and expose that raw, aching need for grace buried deep inside. You only truly realize you've hit rock bottom when you discover the unshakeable Rock beneath you. Pain isn't the enemy. It's

the catalyst—the fire that burns away everything false, leaving behind only what's real.

Strength doesn't come from a life of ease.
It erupts from weakness, from struggle. Remember Paul's "thorn in the flesh"? It wasn't
a curse. It was the chisel that shaped him.
God's words to him ring out even now: "My
grace is sufficient for you, for My power is
made perfect in weakness." Paul didn't shrink
back in fear. He stood tall, fierce, and unshak-
en because true power doesn't come from
control. It comes from surrender.

Breakdowns? They demolish the idols we
secretly worship—control, success, relation-

ships, even our own self-righteousness. They corner us, force us to confront the fragile human beneath all the façades. Without them, we'd never face just how desperately we need a Savior. The world tells us to hide our weaknesses. But Christ? He says, "Bring them into the light."

Look at Peter. He was so sure of himself, boasting, "I'll never deny You." But when fear hit, he crumbled. His denials echoed like gunshots in the dark. His tears weren't just about guilt; they were like acid, melting away his arrogance. And in that brokenness, Jesus rebuilt him—not as a man who never failed, but as someone who knew grace in the most intimate way possible.

Loss feels final, doesn't it? Losing your identity, security, health—it's like watching everything slip through your fingers. But in God's hands, loss isn't the end. It's fertile ground. Look at David's Psalms. They're soaked with raw, desperate cries: "Out of the depths, I cry to You, O Lord." That's not defeat. That's faith forged in the darkness.

When everything falls apart, we're left staring at this brutal truth—nothing we achieve can fill that God-shaped void inside us. It's a painful revelation, but it's in surrender that transformation begins. Paul had all the credentials, all the achievements, but after Damascus, he called them rubbish. Why? Because knowing Christ eclipsed everything else.

Breakdowns feel like endings. But with Christ, they're ground zero for new beginnings—beauty rising from ashes, joy replacing mourning, praise pushing out despair. Even Jesus broke. In Gethsemane, He sweat blood, His cry piercing the night: "Father, if You're willing, take this cup—but not My will, Yours be done." The Son of God, vulnerable, wrestling with what lay ahead. But it was in that surrender that victory was born.

Corinth was a mess—divided, immoral, immature. Paul didn't just shake his finger at them in judgment. He injected hope into their chaos. God chooses the foolish to shame the wise, the weak to shame the strong.

Breakthrough isn't about getting back to the way things were. It's about becoming someone new entirely. A caterpillar doesn't "fix" itself; it dissolves in darkness, only to emerge as something transformed, something beautiful.

Think about the prodigal son. He hit rock bottom, feeding pigs, starving, broken. His breakdown cracked his heart wide open to repentance. And when he returned home, his father didn't scold him or lecture him. No, he ran—arms wide open, grace spilling over.

Paul's chains? They didn't bind his spirit. Prison walls couldn't contain his purpose. His breakthroughs weren't tied to his circumstances; they were anchored in unshakable faith. Breakdowns birth empathy. Scarred souls become comforters, carrying echoes of God's faithfulness. Growth demands breaking, pruning. It's painful, but it's necessary.

So, maybe shift the question from "Why me?" to "What's God forging in me?" Pain doesn't disappear, but purpose has a way of reframing it. Paul's life after Damascus wasn't easy, but it was electrified with purpose. Suffering didn't define him—Christ did. He found contentment in all things because his strength wasn't his own.

Breakdowns strip away all the noise. What's left? Clarity. God's presence. And that's enough.

The path from breakdown to breakthrough isn't tidy. It's messy, filled with setbacks. But every stumble is part of the transformation. God doesn't waste pain. He molds it, carves purpose from it, creates testimonies from our scars.

Like Mary, like Paul, our breakdowns aren't graves—they're birthing rooms for authentic faith. When we hit the end of ourselves, that's when we crash into grace.

So, if you're breaking right now, hold on. Christ is near. Your breakthrough might be just one cry away.

CHAPTER 15

THE BREAKTHROUGH

"But thanks be to God, who gives us the victory through our Lord Jesus Christ." (1 Corinthians 15:57, ESV)

Let's talk about breakthrough—not as something passive or distant, but as an active, fierce engagement with the very trials and limitations that try to hold us back. Break-through with Christ isn't just about hoping things get better. It's about experiencing the moment when the heavy chains of fear, doubt, and despair shatter under the weight of divine intervention. Christ doesn't just sit beside us offering comfort in our struggles; He equips us with the power to overcome them. His victory over sin and death isn't just a historical fact—it's the foundation of our personal triumphs today. Through relentless faith, we don't just endure; we seize the victory He has already secured, turning our darkest seasons into powerful testimonies of His grace and strength.

Breaking through with Christ means facing adversity head-on with the full confidence of His presence. Imagine standing eye-to-eye with the impossible and boldly declaring, "Nothing will be impossible with God" (Luke 1:37, ESV). This kind of faith doesn't whisper timidly in the face of despair. It roars, pushing past human limitations into the realm of the miraculous. It's the refusal to accept defeat, fueled by the unshakable belief that the same power that raised Jesus from the dead is alive and active within us (Romans 8:11, ESV).

But let's be real—breakthrough isn't just about winning external battles. It's also about conquering the internal ones. It's about the transformation that happens deep within, where fear gives way to courage, and human weakness is overshadowed by divine strength. Every day, when we surrender to Christ's lordship, His truth dismantles the lies that try to imprison our minds. Our strength doesn't come from ourselves; it comes from leaning fully into Him. In Christ, breakthrough isn't some distant hope on the horizon—it's our present reality, waiting to be claimed by faith and lived out with boldness.

Some days feel like a relentless battle, don't they? Every breath feels like a small victory against the tide. The weight of life presses down, making it hard to even stand. And then there are those deceptively quiet days, filled with an eerie stillness—like the calm before a storm. But no matter how fierce the fight feels, the outcome never changes. Victory isn't some distant wish; it's a sealed, irrevocable truth. Not because of our strength, but because of Jesus' finished work on the cross.

He triumphed once and for all, and that victory is ours.

We're not just participants in life's battles; we are warriors equipped with the certainty of triumph. Knowing this shifts everything. Desperation turns into fierce confidence. Every act of endurance becomes more than just surviving—it becomes an anthem of worship. Our struggles aren't meaningless; they are sacred ground where our faith is forged and refined.

God never promised us an easy road. He didn't sugarcoat the journey or hide the struggles we'd face. But He did guarantee success—not the fragile kind the world offers, but the eternal, unshakable kind. When we anchor ourselves to that promise, we stop measuring progress by the sting of our wounds or the depth of our scars. Instead, we measure it against His unwavering faithfulness. Remember, at the cross, Jesus didn't whisper, "I'm almost there." He declared with authority, "It is finished." That wasn't resignation. It was the triumphant cry of a King declaring absolute, unchallenged victory. That victory isn't just a concept; it's our reality to live, breathe, and fight from.

Yes, trials will come. Waves will crash, and darkness will try to creep in. But we stand firm because we know the ending. We are not victims of circumstance—we are victors navigating temporary storms with eternal assurance. Jesus didn't just pull us out of the pit; He armed us with heavenly armor. He gave us His Spirit—a roaring fire within us. His Word—a sword sharper than any earthly blade. His people—a battalion of faith warriors. His promises—unbreakable oaths sealed with His blood.

Endurance isn't about being worn down. It's the badge of the faithful. Every time you choose to rise when it's easier to fall, every time you speak truth when silence feels safer, every time you love when it hurts—that's you shouting into the darkness, "My God is still worthy!" Every refusal to quit is a declaration: "His promises are still standing—unshaken and undefeated."

I've been through seasons where worship felt like a faint whisper, where prayers echoed back hollow, and hope seemed fragile. But I pressed on—not because I was strong, but because I clung to the One who never lets go. That wasn't just survival; that was worship.

Every shaky step forward was a testament to His sufficiency.

Teach your children this sacred truth: Perseverance isn't weakness; it's spiritual strength. It's having the courage to stand when your legs tremble, to believe when doubt screams, to love when your heart aches. Every act of endurance is a bold declaration of faith—a sermon without words, louder and more powerful than anything you could say.

Hope isn't wishful thinking; it's a battle cry. It defies despair, anchors us when everything else shakes, and roots itself not in fleeting circumstances, but in the unshakable reality of the resurrection. I've clung to that hope in sterile hospital rooms, amidst heartbreak's wreckage, and in the suffocating silence of unanswered prayers. And every single time, hope reminded me, "This isn't the end. The Author of your story is still writing, and His pen never slips."

Encourage your children to hope fiercely. To expect redemption around every corner. To believe that restoration isn't just possible—it's promised. Hope carries light, and in the battle between light and darkness, light never loses.

Endurance isn't about brute strength; it's living evidence of real, raw faith. It's proof that our roots run deep even when storms rage. That trust doesn't depend on sunny skies but thrives in the middle of tempests. Our endurance flows not from willpower, but from the very presence of God pulsing through our hearts.

God doesn't demand perfection from us. He asks for persistence. Show up—even if you're battle-scarred and weary. Keep showing up. That consistency becomes a witness, a beacon declaring, "Grace holds. Faith works. Jesus is enough."

Paul's words weren't just poetic musings; they were battle cries: "I have fought the good fight, finished the race, and kept the faith." That's not just his story—it's our blueprint. The finish line isn't just heaven someday. It's the legacy we create in every life we touch, every truth we speak, every act of love we give.

But let's be honest—fatigue will lie to you. It'll whisper, "You've done enough," "You're insignificant," "You can't keep going." Don't believe it. When your spirit feels faint, let Scripture roar louder. It doesn't just suggest perseverance—it commands it because the harvest is coming. That's not just motivation; it's a battle plan for victory.

Revelation doesn't end with uncertainty. It crescendos in glory—Jesus reigning supreme, evil crushed, every tear wiped away. That's not wishful thinking. It's the finale of a story already written, already secured.

So don't just hope for victory—live from it. Every prayer, every act of sacrifice, every breath of obedience is part of the grand, triumphant narrative of eternity.

Teach your children to walk with victory etched into their souls. To speak with conviction. To love without hesitation. To stand firm even when the ground shakes. When they know the ending, fear loses its grip on the middle.

You are never alone. Heaven is cheering you on. In the silence, in the struggle, in the solitude—God is near. His Spirit burns within you. His promises are your unshakable foundation.

Victory isn't pending. It's proclaimed. Not because we're flawless, but because Jesus finished the work flawlessly. Not because we're mighty, but because He is the Almighty.

So rise up. Pray like heaven hears—because it does. Worship like chains break—because they do. Stand firm, not as fragile beings, but as conquerors clothed in Christ. The battle is fierce, but the ending is radiant.

Instill in your children the grit to persist, the courage to believe, the audacity to hope. Success isn't stumbled upon—it's carved out through relentless faith. And that faith shapes lives filled with resilience, purpose, and eternal significance.

The war is won. The mission continues. And you, dear warrior, are part of the greatest story ever told. This is your breakthrough.

CONCLUSION

Y ou know, for me, this isn't just a bunch of ideas thrown together. It's personal. It's my lifeline. It's how I've come to truly know Jesus—not as some distant figure, but as someone real, present, and powerful in my everyday life. He's not far away, unreachable, or silent. No, He's here, right now, speaking to me, moving in my life, transforming me from the inside out. I feel His presence in every heartbeat, and His grace fills up every broken, hurting part of me.

When I sat down to write these words, I wasn't fearless. In fact, I wrestled with a lot of fear—fear of being vulnerable, fear of rejection, fear of putting my faith out there boldly for everyone to see. But here's the thing: fear doesn't get the final say. It doesn't own me. The very principles Jesus taught us are the tools we use to break those chains. His truth cuts through the lies that hold us back. His love tears down the walls we build. His light shines into every dark corner, and in that light, we find courage we never knew we had.

Breakthrough isn't always dramatic. It's not like a sudden loud thunderclap marking one defining moment. In reality, it's a process—a slow, steady, relentless process. It's a sacred unraveling of old habits, old fears, and a holy rebuilding of who we're meant to be. It's about letting go of what's holding us back, daring to begin again, even when life feels like walking through thick fog. It's grace picking us up when we fall, rest giving us strength in the middle of struggles, and learning to hold both deep longing and profound contentment at the same time. Jesus never asked us to be perfect. He simply says, "Walk with Me." That's where freedom begins to breathe and thrive.

If you've ever felt the crushing weight of lies lifted off your shoulders or that soul-deep relief that comes with forgiveness wrapping around you like the warmest embrace, I get it. I've been there too. I've felt that same freedom. Knowing who you are in Christ and standing tall in that spiritual authority—it's not just noise or hype. It's real. It's raw. It's practical. These are sacred tools God has placed in our hands because His love knows no limits. You are not forgotten. You are chosen. You are equipped for this journey.

This isn't about trying harder or chasing some unattainable goal. Transformation comes from walking in unshakable truth, loving fiercely and without reservation, and always remembering who you are and who created you. Life will bring storms—that's a given. But when they come, stand firm. Not on your own fragile strength, but anchored in the unbreakable grace that surrounds you, holds you, and refuses to ever let you go.

If something in these words stirred your heart—maybe a flicker of hope, a rise of conviction, a whisper of healing—don't ignore it. That's the Spirit, alive and active, nudging you closer to God's heart. Pause. Breathe it in. Let it sink deep into your soul. Let it spark the next chapter of your story. And when it does, share it. Let your life shine like a beacon reflecting God's relentless goodness.

Even when doubts creep in like unwelcome shadows, you'll know where to turn. You've heard that still, small voice that speaks peace into your chaos. You've met the Shepherd who sees you, even in the hidden places, and stays right there with you. That connection—that sacred understanding—that's your breakthrough. That's your anchor.

So now, speak life. Declare truth. Let your story echo God's boundless love. You don't need to have all the answers—I certainly don't. But we know the One who does. Stay close to Him. Lean in. Because that's where breakthrough doesn't just happen—it multiplies.

And this? This isn't the end. It's just the beginning. Old chains are breaking. New doors are opening. Jesus isn't done with us. He's just getting started. The road ahead might twist and turn, filled with uncertainties, but it's soaked in promise. Keep moving forward. Stay honest. Stay grounded. Keep your eyes fixed on Him.

Breakthrough isn't just a fleeting moment. It's a posture, a lifestyle, a heartbeat. You're not walking this road alone. Start right here, right now. Kneel before God with open hands and a surrendered heart. In that sacred surrender, breakthrough doesn't just visit—it takes root. This is the rescue. This is the revolution. This is abundant, unshaken life.

REDEEMED GRACE PUBLICATIONS

LOVE - COURAGE - FAITH

www.ingramcontent.com/pod-product-compliance
Lightning Source LLC
Chambersburg PA
CBHW021232130626
46554CB00004B/1457